the toddler's chant

the toddler's chant

selected poems
1998-2008
&
some new ones since

3rd edition

Stanford M. Forrester/*sekiro*

Stark Mountain Press
Colrain, Massachusetts

the toddler's chant

selected poems 1998-2008
&
some new ones since

3rd edition

Printed & Published in the USA
by Stark Mountain Press

ISBN 978-0-9832298-4-1

Stark Mountain Press
Colrain, Massachusetts

for holy fools everywhere

It is a bit embarassing to have been concerned with the human problem all one's life and find at the end that one has no more to offer by way of advice than 'try to be a little kinder.'

— Aldous Huxley

out of season —
the haiku poet tells us
to ignore the frog

old jazz record
a scratch
    improvises

down south —
the waitress with a bee-hive
calls me *honey*

doctor's office —
the Dixie cup
half full, half empty

soccer match —
the player named Gandhi
with the most fouls

Halloween party —
noticing **Death**
put on a few pounds

Halloween 1974

When I was really little it was the costumes that made me look forward to Halloween. I could be Spider-Man, the Werewolf or countless other beings with superpowers. As I got older it wasn't the costumes that attracted me to the holiday as much as the thought of being at a party with *girls*. The night offered more opportunities than most to actually kiss a girl, and in costume I was willing to take the chance.

       spin the bottle —
       every turn
       I get myself

x-mas tree ornaments . . .
the jolly buddha
bends a branch

New Year's Eve —
not liking my fortune
i buy another

no need
to be reminded —
April Fool's Day

clowning around

clown:
out of his makeup . . .
out of himself   *for NV*

clown lunchroom
the pies
all whipped cream

clown school —
getting sent
to the principal's office

April Fool's Day
the clown school
closed

playing army . . .
   the little boys fight
over who's dead

bits of paper & smoke . . .
a bottle rocket
after the bang

plastic dolls   in an old box   topless, bottomless

summer afternoon . . .
losing the superball
on the first bounce

backyard sun shower . . .
the windchime song
changes with each cloud

23

cereal box —
the **toy submarine**
at the bottom

5th grade —
a love note folded
100 times

e-mail affair —
her attachment
gives me a virus

motel stillness . . .
the bed
out of quarters

the moon & stars
given away . . .
old love letter

burning an old love letter . . .
a moth
circles my way

candle light —
the moth
my only muse

falling for
   the flame trick again . . .
      me & the moth

ocean waves ~
her
deep
wet
kiss

end of summer . . .
tracing her tan line
into autumn

petals fall
and the thorns stay . . .
summer roses

Maine woods —
the only preacher
jack-in-the-pulpit

below
heaven
gravity

daylight . . .
no one notices
the firefly

climbing
the mountain too . . .
wild blueberries

they actually
are pretty quiet . . .
wild flowers

wordless each poem . . .
a trail
of birches

autumn chill —
a stick bug stirs
from the tinder

end of October . . .
   shaking the seeds
      out of the cosmos

the haiku manual of Icarus
& other myths

forgotten temple . . .
a yellow flower
offers itself

ancient grove . . .
an orange falls
into its shadow

Acropolis —
light leaking
from a cracked urn

temple ruins . . .
pillars hold up
the Athens sky

grains of sand . . .
each ant
a Sisyphus

Athens wind —
    the fish market
    the incense vendor

morning agenda
— see Zeus
— see Tom*

*H. F. Noyes

that Orpheus —
always looking
back

afternoon light . . .
a single bird singing
in the amphitheatre

a goldfinch flies
into blinding sun —
thoughts of Icarus

sunflower field . . .
playing hide-n-seek
with the cyclops

Sunflower,
  you be the sun
    & i'll be Icarus

Delphi —
the Greek
tour guide
calls
the Roman
ruins
new

tum
   bled
      pillars
crook
   ed
      sha
dows

Poseidon's Temple
below the precipice
a chorus of waves

cold Aegean sun —
the temple
half stone, half shadow

These poems were written in Greece during the first month of 2004.

Bangalore, India

Shiva's Temple —
a toddler chants along
in baby talk

taxi ride traffic —
letting the septic tank truck
have its way

Hindu temple —
a stray dog runs off
with my shoe

motel room —
my last night in India spent
with a mosquito

These poems were written in the second month of 2008 while participating in the World Haiku Festival in Bangalore, India.

target practice

the master
missing every shot . . .
Zen archery

        asking the instructor
        for a bigger target —
        Zen archery

Zen archery —
shooting an apple
off my mind

        Zen archery —
        aimed for my mind, but hit
        someone else's

Zen archery letting go

        the point
        aimless —
        Zen archery

Zen archery —
after practice
plucking out all the arrows

Zen retreat —
practicing emptiness
in a crowded room

Zen meditation —
  emptying my mind
    when no one is looking

Zen retreat —
i awaken
with a cup of coffee

insy or outsy
belly button
either way, no attachments

Zen garden —
the monk rakes over
his thoughts

motionless   or not the snail

one perfect ensō
after another . . .
autumn rain

holy water . . .
a drop of rain
in Buddha's belly button

meditation hall . . .
an ant carries away
my concentration

for J.W. Hackett

wind, seed, straw, & feather

autumn colors —
the scarecrow's shirt
nicer than mine

October wind . . .
the leaves & wicker basket
both blow away

end of autumn . . .
finding myself
in a field of thistle

godless month . . .
i save
a pumpkin seed

first snow . . .
the scarecrow wears
a new coat

winter wind   a crow leaves behind   its caw

April morning   the crow too   has a song

when a scarecrow   isn't   the last straw

every
season
crows

morning light —
the cherry tree's shadow
also blossoms

cherry blossom festival —
a crabapple tree
gets the most attention

blossom tea —
the geisha drinks
her reflection

sunlit pond
the echo
of each tadpole

Japanese garden . . .
each firefly
a lantern

Japanese hotel —
Gideon & Buddha share
the same drawer

windy afternoon —
at the temple gate
the Wind God's grin

Jizō altar   the faded face   of a Kewpee doll

temple ruins . . .
pieces of a buddha
still praying

summer heat . . .
i paint the word *breeze*
on my paper fan

& some new poems since

walking home   the stone in my shoe   i don't take out

autumn
sky

my
depression
too

full
of
crows

end
of
October

the
scare
crow

crow
less

a cup of coffee
and a handful of meds . . .
Monday's breakfast

cup of tea —
the moon still
until i sip it

winding brook —
saying something different
at each turn

rainy
day . . .

i
only
saved

my
mistakes

a stone
i saved
casting stones

my haiku about the moon —
outdone
by the moon

could
have

called
it
water —

thin
soup

at the start
of National Poetry Month —
April Fool's Day

for Tom Painting

soup de jour

potluck dinner —
each poet brings
stone soup

stone soup —
the poets
compare recipes

poets' cook-off
can't tell my stone soup
from the others'

the other poets
ask for my recipe —
stone soup

clunk sound!
dipping the ladle into
the stone soup

last night's stone soup
nothing left
but pebbles . . .

Stone Soup is an old folk tale in which a hungry stranger persuades an elderly woman in a small town to give him food. When writing these poems, Ann McGovern's 1967 version, published by Scholastic, came to mind.

loneliness   sitting by a fire   that won't stay lit

dinnertime —
the old cat regains
his hearing

November walk . . .
settling for what's left
of the bittersweet

hototogisu —
   you're probably saying
      the same thing about me

knock-knock joke   the woodpecker tells   only the first half

reruns   of Saturday morning cartoons   2AM

more
snow
more
snow

my old
age
shaved
off

until
the next
morning

death poem —
my father left
without one

Penn Station —
on the loudspeaker, a call
for my dead father's town

a Mason Jar full of wildflowers —
the thistle
always lasts the longest

day moon
the poem sounded better
last night

October sky . . .
not a single cloud shaped
like Buddha

About the Author

Stanford M. Forrester/*sekiro* is a poet, past president of the Haiku Society of America, and editor of *bottle rockets: a collection of short verse* for the past 20 years. Forrester's haigo, his Japanese pen name, is *sekiro* which means dew on a stone. He currently lives in a "fleeting world" that some call Connecticut.

Acknowledgments

acorn, Asahi Shimbun/International Herald Tribune (Japan), Boston Haiku Soc. News, Chiyo's Corner, dew-on-line (England), Frogpond, Haiku Canada, Haiku, Haiku Headlines, Haiku Presence (England), Hermitage (Romania), HNA 2003 Anthology, Hummingbird, Ko (Japan), Lilliput Review, Mariposa, Mayfly, Modern Haiku, Nisqually Delta Review, noon (Japan), Paper Wasp (Australia), *Rabbit Ears* (New York Quarterly) Raw NerVZ (Canada), simply haiku, snapshots (England), South by Southeast, still (England), tinywords.com, Vancouver Cherry Blossom Festical (Canada), White Lotus, and the World Haiku Club Anthology (England & Japan).